ESSENTIAL SUCCULENTS FOR BEGINNERS

The Ultimate Guide To Growing Beautiful & Long-Lasting Cacti And Succulents With A Directory of 300+ Common Species And Varieties

Roy A. Starr

CHAPTER 1

INTRODUCTION TO SUCCULENTS

Appreciating the Hardy Beauty of Nature:

Succulents are hardy and fascinating denizens of the wide world of botanical marvels, drawing in visitors of all experience levels. Beginners should choose these charming plants since they are a great introduction to the fascinating world of gardening and are well-known for requiring little maintenance.

They are a broad category of plants distinguished by their ability to retain water in certain tissues. The name "succulent" is derived from the Latin word "succus," which means juice or sap. These amazing creatures have adapted to live in dry environments via evolution, showing off a special ability to store moisture. They are ideal companions for those who are beginning to learn how to cultivate since their leaves, stems, or roots often include fleshy characteristics that allow them to withstand prolonged periods of dryness.

Why Should Beginners Use Succulents?

Succulents are kind tutors for individuals venturing into the realm of greenery for the first time. Their minimal care needs and tolerant nature make them a great place to start for those who want to develop a green thumb. Succulents tolerate occasional neglect fairly well, unlike many delicate plants that need careful care. As their resilient charges thrive under their care, this forgiving attitude not only offers a safety net for novices but also cultivates a feeling of success.

Succulents' Resistant Nature:

Many other plant species would struggle to survive in the severe circumstances that succulents have evolved to withstand thanks to their clever processes of adaptation. They can withstand protracted dry spells because of their ability to store water and special metabolic adaptations. Succulents are more tolerant of changes in watering schedules, which lowers the margin for error for inexperienced gardeners.

This attribute results in an accommodating learning curve for beginners. Compared to more demanding plants, succulents are less likely to suffer much from the odd slip-up in watering schedules or changes in solar exposure. This kind of attitude gives beginners a feeling of self-assurance and achievement when they see their succulents flourishing despite any mistakes.

Delicious Symphony: A Rainbow of Special Qualities

Succulents are fascinating plants with many special qualities that make them stand out among other botanical marvels. Their capacity to store water is one of their most distinguishing qualities. Water conservation is a skill that succulents have perfected, retaining valuable liquids in their leaves, stems, and roots. Because of their adaption, they can withstand extended periods without rain, which makes them experts at surviving in even the most hostile conditions.

Succulents also display a wide range of sizes, colours, and forms, transforming any garden into a living work of art. Succulents provide an abundance of creative expression opportunities, ranging from the sculptural allure of Aloe Vera to the flowing grace of Burro's Tail (Sedum morganianum). Their distinct aesthetics provide people with a way to curate plants that reflect their individuality while also beautifying environments.

The Easy-To-Maintain Style:

Succulents are praised not just for their ability to hold onto water but also for their minimal care needs. These hardy plants thrive in many different environments, from sunny windowsills to outdoor gardens, and they adjust to new circumstances with ease. They are adaptable companions for both indoor and outdoor environments, providing a flexible canvas for growing greens because of their tolerance for a variety of temperatures and light conditions.

It takes no expertise to care for succulents; everyone can do it. Hardy plants that thrive with little care and provide a sense of organic beauty to any setting. Succulents happily adapt to your lifestyle, requiring just occasional watering and well-draining soil to flourish, whether you're a busy professional or a student managing a rigorous schedule.

Ability to Adjust to Diverse Environments:

Succulents' flexibility in a variety of living settings is another appealing feature for novices. Succulents are adaptable to almost any kind of habitat, whether you have a large garden or an apartment with little outside space. Succulents are adaptable to almost any kind of container, so they work well in hanging planters, terrariums, and potted gardens alike.

This flexibility is not limited by geography. Because succulents can grow in both indoor and outdoor environments, gardeners may use them in any climate. For those in colder locations, keeping succulents inside enables the delight of caring for these plants year-round, bringing a touch of nature into the heart of any house.

Visual Appeal and Variety:

Succulents' striking variety and visual appeal capture novices even beyond their utilitarian benefits. For individuals who are interested in learning more about the world of plants, the succulent kingdom's wide variety of forms, hues, and sizes is an eye-opening experience. Succulents provide a canvas for creative expression in gardening, from the elaborate rosettes of Echeveria to the architectural grandeur of Agave.

The visual attraction of succulents also extends to their ability to match diverse design types.

There is a delicious selection that may easily fit into your selected theme, whether you want a more eclectic and bohemian look or a contemporary, minimalist one. Because of their versatility, succulents may be cultivated by novices to express their interests and customize their green areas.

Connecting with Nature:

For many beginner gardeners, the experience is about developing a stronger connection with nature as much as with caring for plants. Succulents encourage people to get up close and personal with the intricate details of plant life because of their fascinating morphologies and development patterns. Taking care of succulents turns into a peaceful activity that provides a break from the stress of everyday life.

We shall explore the unique varieties of succulents that are especially good for novices in the next chapters. Every succulent type has something special to offer, from the hardy Snake

Plant to the enchanting Aloe Vera with its calming gel. You will learn more about the needs for each species' upkeep, methods of propagation, and possible applications as we delve further into each one.

Succulents are, after all, both wonderful companions for beginners and wonderful representatives of the fascinating world of plants. Together, we will explore the mysteries of succulent culture as we set out on this adventure, making sure that your gardening endeavours are not only fruitful but also brimming with the delight of tending to life in all of its robust and interesting forms.

In conclusion, individuals who are starting the exciting path of caring for plants are welcomed with open arms by succulents. Their distinct qualities combined with elegant, low-maintenance design make them a wonderful option for novices as well as a captivating accent to any landscape. Discovering the world of succulents will open your eyes to a thriving plant community that is eager to share its resilience and beauty, turning your area into a natural wonderland.

- **Revealing The Special Qualities of Succulents:**

1. Proficiency in Water Storage:

Succulents' ability to store water, which has evolved to enable plants to flourish in situations where water is scarce, is a key component of their appeal. This characteristic is most seen in their luscious leaves, stems, or roots, which serve as water-storing reservoirs. Succulents may survive for extended periods without rain thanks to these reservoirs because they can use the moisture they have saved to stay alive.

The anatomical modifications that allow succulent species to store water differ. Water-absorbing tissues, for instance, are housed in the leaves of the iconic Sempervivum and

Echeveria rosettes, creating a compact structure that reduces water loss through evaporation. Similar to succulents, cacti are characterized by modified leaves with spines that decrease surface area and, thus, water loss.

For beginners, it is essential to comprehend how succulents store water. It not only explains why they withstand sporadic watering but also directs appropriate maintenance procedures. Overwatering is a frequent mistake that many plants make, but it may be especially harmful to succulents because it throws off their delicate water balance. Beginner gardeners may create a healthy connection with their succulents by understanding the nuances of water storage and giving them exactly the appropriate quantity of moisture.

2. Low Need for Maintenance:

The fact that succulents need less care is a major attraction for novices who want to become plant parents. These hardy plants are gentle companions for beginners who are acclimating to harsh environments since they have evolved to flourish there. Their low-maintenance nature is attributed to a variety of traits.

a. Requirements for Infrequent Watering:

Succulents have developed to need less regular irrigation than their drier brethren. Their watering requirements are a reflection of their capacity to store water, which enables them to withstand dry times. The fact that succulents like deep, infrequent waterings tends to reassure novice gardeners. This method encourages healthy root growth and avoids problems related to overwatering by imitating the natural rainfall patterns of dry locations.

b.Adaptability to Less-than-Optimal Conditions:

Succulents are very resilient to less-than-ideal growth circumstances. These hardy plants thrive in conditions where their soil quality is subpar or in places with intense sunshine. This feature is quite helpful for novice gardeners who may not have the ideal setup. While it is known that succulents may grow in a variety of lighting environments, the majority of species prefer bright, indirect sunshine.

c. Minimal Need for Nutrients:

In terms of dietary supplements, succulents are not picky. They can tolerate nutrient-poor soils, however they do benefit from a balanced fertilizer throughout their active growth season. For novices, the care regimen is made simpler by the simplicity of the dietary requirements. It also implies that, in contrast to plants with greater nutritional requirements, succulents may flourish in container gardens with well-draining soil and need less regular repotting.

d. Flexibility for Indoor Lifestyle:

Succulents are an alluring option for those who live in areas with severe weather conditions or have limited outdoor space. Numerous types of succulents grow well inside, flourishing on shelves, windowsills, and in ornamental arrangements. This flexibility encourages a connection with nature even in urban environments and brings the pleasure of gardening inside.

e. Resistance to Pests and Diseases

Because of their distinct morphologies and molecular makeup, succulents possess innate resistance to numerous pests and illnesses. Although no plant is completely impervious, succulents' strong defenses lessen the chance of infections. Beginners are less burdened by this resistance, enabling them to concentrate on the pleasures of cultivation rather than having to constantly watch out for typical garden pests.

Succulents' low-maintenance qualities essentially allow novices to cultivate with confidence from the start. These plants' ability to be understanding acts as a buffer against unavoidable errors, enabling people to improve as gardeners. As we continue our investigation of essential succulents, we will go more deeply into particular maintenance techniques to make sure that you not only grow healthy succulents but also gain a greater understanding of their special characteristics, which make them the perfect companions for beginners in the horticultural world.

CHAPTER 2

TYPES, ORIGIN, FEATURES AND USES OF ESSENTIAL SUCCULENTS

- ## Aloe Vera(Aloe barbadensis miller)

Aloe Vera is a species of succulent plant in the Aloe genus. We call it Aloe barbadensis miller in scientific parlance. Aloe vera is widely cultivated, therefore its precise origin is unknown, however, it is said to have started on the Arabian Peninsula. The plant is now widespread across the globe, especially in tropical and subtropical areas, having adapted to a variety of conditions.

Features:

Aloe Vera's characteristic rosette of thick, meaty, lance-shaped leaves is what gives it its unmistakable appearance. These leaves may reach a length of two feet and are usually green or gray-green.

Gel-filled Leaves: Known for its many medical uses, the leaves contain a transparent, gel-like material. Antioxidants, vitamins, minerals, and amino acids abound in this gel.

Serrated Edges: The leaves often have serrated edges, and there may be tiny white dots on their surface. Depending on the Aloe Vera cultivar, these serrations may have varying degrees of severity.

Cultivation:

Adaptability: Aloe Vera is well-known for being drought-tolerant and hardy. It needs plenty of sunshine and well-draining soil to flourish both inside and outdoors.
Propagation: Offsets, seeds, or leaf cuttings may all be used to spread the plant. It's generally

low-maintenance and resistant to many pests and illnesses.

Uses:

Aloe Vera gel is well-recognized for having medicinal qualities. It is often used topically to relieve and cure small wounds, sunburns, and skin irritations. Compounds with antibacterial and anti-inflammatory properties are included in the gel.

Skincare: Because of its hydrating and skin-soothing properties, aloe vera is often used as a component in skincare products such as lotions, creams, and gels.

Digestive Aid: Aloe Vera juice is used by certain individuals due to its possible digestive advantages. It is crucial to use it with caution, however, since too much of it might have a laxative effect.

Cosmetic Uses: Due to its alleged ability to support healthy hair, aloe vera is a common ingredient in a variety of cosmetics, including shampoos and conditioners.

Precautions:

Although aloe vera is typically safe to use topically, allergies may occur in some people. Patch testing should be done before applying significant quantities.

Take Care When Orally Consumed: Compounds in aloe vera latex, which is located immediately under the plant's epidermis, may have a laxative effect. Oral ingestion should thus be done carefully and under supervision.

In summary, aloe vera is unique not only because of its striking look but also because of its many applications in medicine, healthcare, and cosmetics. It has become a mainstay in families throughout, valued for its natural therapeutic benefits.

- **Echeveria Succulents (Echeveria Spp.)**

Succulent plants of the genus Echeveria, belonging to the family Crassulaceae, are widely distributed across the Americas. These plants, which are native to Mexico, Central America, and northwest South America, do best in dry, well-drained soil that receives plenty of sunshine. Atanasio Echeverría y Godoy, a Mexican botanical artist, is honoured by the genus name.

Features:

Rosette Formation: Depending on the species, echeveria's characteristic rosette-shaped arrangement of leaves may vary in size, shape, and colour.

Foliage: To help retain water, leaves often have a waxy covering and are meaty. Echeveria leaves come in a wide range of colours, including purple, blue, pink, and even black.

Blooms: On tall stalks, echeverias bear beautiful bell-shaped blooms. The blooming season, which typically lasts from late spring to early summer, has vivid hues like red, orange, pink, or yellow.

Size: Echeveria plants come in a variety of sizes, from compact, little species to bigger, more sprawling kinds.

There are several species and hybrids in the genus, and each has distinct qualities of its own. Echeveria agavoides (Lipstick Echeveria), Echeveria pulidonis, and Echeveria elegans (Mexican Snowball) are common species.

Growth and Maintenance:

Sunshine: Bright, indirect sunshine is ideal for echeveria growth. While strong, direct sunlight may burn, insufficient light can cause leaves to expand.

Soil: Echeverias need well-draining soil. To avoid waterlogging, a mixture of sand or perlite and cactus potting soil works best.

Watering: Because echeverias can withstand drought, it's important to let the soil dry up in between waterings. Rotten roots might result from overwatering.

Temperature: Although they may withstand brief periods of cold, these succulents love warm weather. Keep them safe from frost since low temperatures might be harmful.

Uses:

Beautifully shaped rosettes on echeverias make them a popular choice for decorative plantings in gardens, rockeries, and containers.

Interior Design: A variety of Echeveria cultivars are great indoor plants that provide a natural element to homes and workplaces.

In landscaping, echeverias are often used in drought-tolerant and xeriscaping projects because of their hardiness and visual attractiveness.

Echeverias are a popular option for succulent displays and gardens; they are often paired with other species that get along well.

In conclusion, aficionados are drawn to Echeveria succulents because of their exquisite rosette forms, a wide range of colours, and tolerance for different climates. These plants are still loved for their distinct appeal and comparatively minimal care needs, whether they are used to decorate landscapes, interior areas, or succulent arrangements.

- **Jade Plant, or Crassula ovata**

The popular succulent Jade Plant, or Crassula ovata in scientific parlance, is a member of the Crassulaceae family. It's a native of South Africa, especially the Eastern Cape, and goes by many names, including Money Plant, Lucky Plant, and Friendship Tree. Its oval-shaped, jade-green leaves are what gave rise to the moniker "Jade Plant".

The roots of jade plants are found in the dry parts of South Africa, where they grow well on rocky soil that drains well. They fit into the succulent category well as they can tolerate dry weather and retain water in their leaves.

Features:

Leaves: The smooth, meaty, glossy leaves of the jade plant are usually elliptic or ovate. They have a characteristic jade-green hue and grow in opposing pairs along the branches; nevertheless, there are varieties with red-edged or variegated leaves.

Growth: The plant reaches up to ten feet in height in its native environment, growing as a shrub or small tree. But when grown inside, it often stays smaller, growing to a height of two to four feet.

Flowers: Under ideal circumstances, jade plants may produce clusters of tiny, star-shaped white or pink flowers. The blossoms enhance the plant's overall appeal even if they are not its main draw.

Hardiness: The Jade Plant, renowned for its adaptability to a range of conditions, is very simple to maintain. For those who are new to the world of succulent gardening, it is often advised.

Growth and Maintenance:

Light: Indirect, bright light is preferred by jade plants. Although they can withstand a certain amount of direct sunshine, too much exposure may cause leaf sunburn.

Watering: The water needs of these succulents are low to moderate. Allow the soil to dry out between waterings to avoid root rot.

Soil: The Jade Plant requires well-draining soil. The best mixture would be cacti or succulents with sand or perlite added.

Uses:

Indoor Décor: Because of their lovely look and low maintenance requirements, jade plants are a popular choice for indoor decorative plantings. They are often used in succulent arrangements or set on windowsills.

Symbolism: The jade plant is seen as a representation of friendship, wealth, and good fortune in many civilizations. Some people think that putting it next to a house or business's entryway would draw prosperity and good vibes.

Bonsai: Due to its natural similarity to small trees, the Jade Plant is also grown as a bonsai. It is appropriate for bonsai aficionados because of its capacity to form a structure resembling a tree.

Feng Shui: The jade plant is said to provide good energy in Feng Shui techniques, particularly when it is positioned in the wealth or prosperity corner of a house or business.

To sum up, the Jade Plant is a popular option among plant aficionados since it is not only an aesthetically beautiful succulent but also has functional use in a variety of situations and cultural value.

- **Stonecrop (Hylotelephium)**

Within the family Crassulaceae, Hylotelephium, or Stonecrop, is a diversified genus of succulent plants. These resilient plants, which are native to Europe and Asia, are today grown all over the globe for their resistance and aesthetic appeal.

Native to Europe and Asia, stonecrop succulents may be found in a variety of environments, such as rocky slopes, cliffs, and meadows. In North America, they have also attained naturalization. Due to morphological and genetic differences, the genus Hylotelephium was reclassified from its previous membership in the Sedum genus.

Features:

1. Foliage: Thick, often vibrant leaves define stonecrop succulents. Depending on the species and type, the leaves may have a range of shapes, including flat, rounded ones or long, pointed ones.

2. Flowers: The plants have star-shaped blooms in a variety of colours, from pink and white to reddish pink. Usually placed in thick clusters, these flowers make eye-catching arrangements.

3. Habit of Growth: The growth patterns of stonecrop succulents are varied and include

clumping mounds, low-growing ground coverings, and taller, erect types. They work well in a variety of garden environments, including rock gardens and container plants, thanks to their diversity.

4. Flexibility: The capacity of Stonecrop succulents to adapt to many environmental circumstances is one of its main traits. They are perfect for low-maintenance landscapes and xeriscaping since they can withstand drought, poor soil, and bright sunshine.

Growth and Maintenance:

1. Garden Ornamental: Because of their eye-catching leaves and blossoms, stonecrop succulents are a popular choice for gardens. They are often used as ground coverings, border plants, and rock gardens. They are useful for landscaping projects because of their capacity to flourish in difficult environments.

2. Gardening in containers: A lot of Stonecrop cultivars are excellent choices for container gardening. They are great options for potted arrangements on balconies, patios, or windowsills because of their durability and small size.

3. Pollinator Attraction: Stonecrop succulents' blooms attract pollinators like bees and butterflies, which enhances a garden's overall biodiversity.

4. Medical Applications: Certain species of Stonecrop are used in several traditional medical practices because of their alleged therapeutic benefits. It's important to remember that there may be variations in the safety and effectiveness of these applications, so speaking with a healthcare provider is recommended.

5. Spread Succulents grown as stonecrops may be reproduced somewhat easily by division, taking stem cuttings, or gathering seeds. This

means that both inexperienced and seasoned gardeners may use them.

In conclusion, a wide variety of species and variations of Hylotelephium succulents, often known as stonecrops, are adaptable and aesthetically pleasing plants. They are a great addition to gardens and landscapes all around the globe because of their decorative value and versatility.

- **Dudleya Spp**

Dudleya originated from North and Central America, the genus Dudleya comprises succulent plants that are mostly found in Mexico and the western United States. The rosette-shaped leaves and distinct growth patterns of these eye-catching succulents are well-known features.

Due to their tolerance to difficult growth environments, they usually live in rocky cliffs, bluffs, and dry settings.

Features:

1. Rosette Form: Dudleya plants often produce visually pleasing rosettes, in which the leaves radiate from a central point.

2. Leaf Varieties: Different species have different leaf shapes and colours. Some have long, finger-like leaves, while others have wider, spoon-shaped leaves.

3. Hues: The visual richness of Dudleya species is enhanced by their range of hues, which include green, blue, gray, and even red tones.

4. Blooms: The plants add a further level to their attractiveness when they develop flower stalks capped with clusters of tiny, star-shaped blooms.

5. Size: Dudleya species come in a variety of sizes, from tiny little rosettes to more expansive, bigger forms.

Care and Cultivation:

1. Sunshine: These succulents need at least six hours of direct sunshine every day to grow.

2. Soil: Dudleya need well-draining soil since they might develop root rot in too wet conditions.

3. Irrigation: They need little irrigation and can withstand droughts. It is best to avoid overwatering to prevent root problems.

4. Temperature: Although dudleya plants can tolerate a wide range of temperatures, most species prefer mild to warm weather.

Uses:

1. Landscaping: Due to its hardiness and visual appeal, Dudleya succulents are a popular option for xeriscaping and rock gardens.

2. Container Gardening: They work well for both indoor and outdoor container gardening because of their small size and eye-catching appeal.

3. Conservation: The loss of habitat and poaching have put several Dudleya species at risk of extinction. These plants are being preserved and protected via efforts.

Conservation problems:

1. Illicit Collection: The horticulture industry's desire for these unusual succulents is driving illicit collection, which puts Dudleya species at risk.

2. Habitat degradation: The wild populations of Dudleya face considerable problems because of urban development and habitat degradation.

In conclusion, Dudleya succulents have ecological significance in addition to being aesthetically pleasing. Preserving the biodiversity of these unusual plants requires an understanding of them and the promotion of their protection.

- **Sempervivum:**

Sempervivum is a genus of succulent plants of the Crassulaceae family. It is sometimes referred to as "hens and chicks" or "houseleeks." The Latin origin of the word "Sempervivum" means "always alive," which reflects the resilience of these plants. They are well-liked for ground coverings, pots, and rock gardens because of their rosette-shaped leaves.

Southern Europe's hilly areas, especially the Alps, Carpathians, and Apennines, are home to Sempervivum. These hardy plants have evolved to a variety of challenging circumstances, such as rocky, arid, and high-altitude settings. Their global cultivation may be attributed, in part, to their hardiness in harsh environments.

Features:

The leaves of Sempervivum plants are usually grouped circularly around a central point, forming compact rosettes. Their growing habit aids in their effective water retention.

Foliage: Sempervivum leaves are waxy or coated in tiny hairs; they are plump and pointy. Different species have different leaf colours, which may range from green to crimson, purple, or even silvery.

Offsets: The capacity of Sempervivum to develop offsets, or "chicks," around the base of the main rosette is one of its distinguishing characteristics. To grow more plants, divide these offsets and plant them separately.

Blooming: The long flower stalks of Sempervivum emerge from the center of the rosette to blossom. Depending on the species, the typically star-shaped blooms might be white, pink, red, or yellow in colour.

Hardiness: These succulents have a reputation for being resilient and cold-tolerant. They can withstand frost and are appropriate for a variety of regions since they are winter-hardy.

Planting and Uses:

Garden Ornamental: Because of their low maintenance requirements and visual appeal, sempervivum is a popular option for ground covers, alpine gardens, and rock gardens.

Container Plants: These plants are perfect for container gardening because of their small size.

Sempervivum gives potted arrangements a distinctive, textural aspect.

Drought resistance: Sempervivum has exceptional drought resistance and is well-adapted to dry environments. They may survive on dry, well-draining soils because of their capacity to retain water in their leaves.

Erosion Control: Because Sempervivum plants grow in mats, their planting in groups may assist prevent soil erosion on rocky or sloping terrain.

Symbiotic interactions: Sempervivum may develop symbiotic partnerships with other plants in their native environment, forming microhabitats that increase biodiversity.

Maintaining Sempervivum:

Sunlight: Full sun is preferred by Sempervivum over partial shade. Compact growth and vivid leaf hues are encouraged by enough sunshine.

Well-Draining Soil: Because they might suffer root rot in excessively wet circumstances, plant them in well-draining soil to avoid waterlogging.

Watering: During the growth season, in particular, let the soil dry up in between applications. Sempervivum may suffer from overwatering.

Propagation: You may either gather seeds from mature plants or separate offsets to propagate Sempervivum.

In summary, Sempervivum succulents are fascinatingly diverse decorative plants with a remarkable range of qualities, as well as hardy survival. Succulent aficionados and gardeners alike love succulents for their hardiness to many climes and their flexibility in a variety of garden settings.

- ## **Snake plant (Sansevieria trifasciata)**

Snake plant is a popular succulent with a distinctive look and many health advantages, is technically known as the Snake Plant. It originated in West Africa, namely in Nigeria and the Congo, but it has now adapted to many temperatures and is grown all over the globe.

Features:

Snake plants feature long, sword-shaped leaves that resemble snakeskin. These leaves are usually dark green with variegated patterns.

Size: They are available in a range of sizes, with some types growing to a height of several feet.

Hardiness: The plant is renowned for its resilience and ability to flourish in low light levels. It's a great option for both outdoor and indoor environments.

Snake plants are well known for their ability to filter the air. They are perfect for enhancing indoor air quality since they can absorb contaminants like benzene and formaldehyde.

Growth and Maintenance:

Light: Snake plants like indirect sunshine, however, they may survive in low light. Their leaves might be scorched by too much direct sunshine.

Watering: Although drought-tolerant, these succulents often get overwatered. Water the soil lightly, letting it dry between applications.

Soil: To avoid root rot, the soil must drain well. Something succulent or cactus-based works well.

Temperature: Although they can tolerate a wide variety of temperatures, snake plants prefer warmer climates. If they are exposed to frost, they could be damaged.

Division: By dividing the offshoots from the primary plant and replanting them, snake plants may be multiplied by division.

Leaf cuttings: To grow new plants, good leaf cuttings may also be rooted in soil or water.

Uses:

Air Purification: They are a useful addition to interior areas because of their capacity to filter the air.

Feng Shui: When planted in appropriate parts of the house, snake plants are said to offer good luck and pleasant energy.

Ornamental: Snake plants are well-liked for their ability to give elegance to houses and workplaces.

Note: Although they are usually safe to consume, snake plants may be poisonous. Keep little children and pets away from them.

The snake plant is a favourite among plant lovers and those looking for an easy-to-care-for green friend since it is a hardy, adaptable succulent with both utilitarian and aesthetic appeal.

- **Haworthia**

Succulent plants of the genus Haworthia are members of the Asphodelaceae family. Native to Southern Africa, namely Namibia and South Africa, these tiny succulents create rosette-shaped plants. Adrian Hardy Haworth, a British botanist, is the name of the genus.

Features:

Form of Rosette: Haworthias usually grow in tense rosettes with spiral-arranged, meaty, pointy leaves.

Leaf Variation: The leaves have a wide range of textures and forms, from solid to transparent, and they often have elaborate patterns and markings.

Haworthia plants come in a range of sizes; some species stay very little, while others may become bigger.
Haworthia leaves come in a variety of colours, including reddish, brown, and green tints.

Inflorescence: Some Haworthia species have thin flower spikes with little tubular blooms, but the foliage is what draws attention.

Growth and Care:

Growing Conditions: Haworthias love bright, indirect light and do best in well-draining soil.

Popular houseplants are well-adapted for indoor growth.

Watering: Due to their desert adaptations, these succulents are delicate to overwatering. Allowing the soil to dry out in between waterings is essential.
Haworthias may be multiplied via leaf cuttings offsets, or pups, which develop around the base of the mother plant.

Container Gardening: Haworthias are often used in terrariums, succulent arrangements, and container gardens because of their small size.

Uses:

Indoor Decor: Haworthias are often employed as ornamental plants to improve the aesthetics of homes and businesses because of their adaptation to indoor environments.

Certain Haworthia species may be used to create rock gardens, which can provide these landscapes with a little more interest and variation.

To assist students and plant enthusiasts learn about the adaptations and care of succulents, these succulents are also used for educational reasons.

The Zebra Plant, Haworthia attenuata, is easily identified by its dark green leaves with white, wavy stripes.

Cooper's Haworthia, or Haworthia cooperi has tightly packed, transparent leaves grouped in a rosette.

Boat Lily, Haworthia cymbiformis: Distinguished by its eye-catching patterns and boat-shaped leaves.

In conclusion, Haworthias are intriguing succulents that have a variety of traits that make them a valued addition to gardens and collections all around the globe. Succulent fans love them for their versatility, distinctive look, and simplicity of maintenance.

- **Agave plants**

Agave plants are found mostly in the hot, dry parts of the Americas, they are succulent perennials that belong to the Agavaceae family. Their main habitats include Mexico, the American Southwest, and portions of Central and South America. The vast collection of plants that make up the genus Agave are all suited to certain environmental circumstances.

Features:

1. Creation of Rosettes: Thick, meaty leaves emanating from a central point characterize the unique rosette growth pattern of agave plants. Depending on the species, the rosette might be small or fairly enormous.

2. Leaves: Succulent agaves have thick, stiff leaves that often have teeth or spines around the margins. The leaves exhibit a broad range of colour and texture, from glossy green to severely textured bluish-grey.

3. Dropping: Because agave plants are monocarpic, they only flower once throughout their lives, usually after many years of development. The blooming stalk is covered with many blooms and may grow to a remarkable height. While offsets or "pups" at the base of the main rosette often die after blooming, they may continue to grow.

4. Arid Environment Adaptations: Agaves can retain water in their leaves, one of several adaptations they have developed to live in dry environments. Additionally, some species have widely dispersed, shallow root systems that effectively absorb rainfall.

Common Species include:

1. Century Plant (Agave americana): Distinguished by its elongated, serrated foliage and soaring blossom stem, this species is well recognized.

2. Parry's Agave, Agave parryi: This species has remarkable blue-grey leaves and is more compact and smaller.

3. Blue agave or Agave tequilana: It is well-known for being the main component used to make tequila. It has long, sharp leaves that are blue-green.

Uses:

1. Recipe: A few agave species are grown specifically for their ability to produce alcoholic drinks like mezcal and tequila, such as Agave tequilana. After being removed from the core, the sap known as aguamiel is fermented.

2. Structure: Historically, agave leaf fibers have been used to make a variety of goods, such as clothes, carpets, and ropes.

3. Garden Design: Owing to their eye-catching appearance and little water needs, several agave species are popular in xeriscaping and dry landscaping.

4. Medical: Certain agave species are thought to offer therapeutic benefits in traditional medicine. It's important to remember that certain uses don't always work, so take caution.

In conclusion, agave succulents are a hardy and varied collection of plants with decorative, commercial, and cultural value. For horticulturists and hobbyists alike, their distinctive growth patterns, adaptation to dry settings, and a multitude of applications make them interesting topics.

- **Kalanchoe (Kalanchoe spp.) Succulents**

The genus Kalanchoe, which belongs to the family Crassulaceae, is a varied collection of succulent plants distinguished by its colourful leaves and persistent, long-lasting blooms.

These are a thorough examination of the many facets of kalanchoe succulents:

Found predominantly in Madagascar, kalanchoes can withstand a wide range of temperatures, from tropical to desert.

Because of their resilience, kalanchoe species have been imported and grown as decorative plants throughout the globe over time.

Features:

Leaf Form: Succulent kalanchoes have a range of leaf sizes, forms, and hues. Ovate, lanceolate, and paddle-shaped leaves are common varieties.

Flowers: The striking clusters of flowers, which might be red, pink, orange, yellow, or white, are one of its distinguishing characteristics. The blooms often resemble tubes.

Growth Habit: Although kalanchoe plants are generally compact, they may grow in a variety of ways, including erect and spreading.

Spread: They spread quickly by seeds, offsets, and leaf cuttings.

Gardening and Maintenance:

Light: Bright, indirect light is ideal for kalanchoe growth. Leaf scorch may result from excessive direct sunlight.

Soil: To avoid root rot, the soil must drain well. Typically, a combination of succulents or cacti is advised.

Watering: Let the soil dry out in between applications; excessive watering might cause problems like root rot.

Temperature: Although they may withstand small variations, these succulents favour mild temperatures.

Some most popular species:

1. Kalanchoe blossfeldiana: One of the most popular types, it's renowned for its vivid blossoms.

2. The fuzzy, silver-green leaves of the panda plant, Kalanchoe tomentosa, are its distinguishing feature.

3. Kalanchoe thyrsiflora, distinguished by its stacked, paddle-shaped leaves.

Uses:

Decorative: The main purpose of kalanchoe cultivation is decorative planting; it may be cultivated in pots or gardens to bring color and texture to interior areas.

Medicinal Purposes: Although certain civilizations have traditionally used some kalanchoe species for therapeutic purposes, care should be taken since they may be harmful.

Challenges:

Potential Toxicity: Several kalanchoe species have substances that, in big enough doses, may be harmful to both people and dogs.

Susceptibility to Disease: A fungus may cause fungal illnesses in vulnerable kinds, and overwatering may cause root rot.

Result: Due to their versatile nature and attractive look, kalanchoe succulents have grown to be a favourite among gardeners. These hardy plants never fail to enthrall, whether they are used as outdoor flourishes or inside companions thanks to their varied range of species and cultivars and distinctive qualities.

- **Apteryx Succulents**

Small succulent plants of the genus Apteryx, usually called Baby Toes, are indigenous to South Africa. Plant aficionados like these interesting succulents, which are members of the Aizoaceae family, for their easy maintenance and distinctive look.

Originated from the Western Cape area of South Africa, Apteryx succulents love rocky, well-draining soils. They thrive in dry settings since their native home is defined by arid circumstances.

Features:

1. Aesthetics: Baby Toes plants get their name from their unusual leaf pairs, which resemble

small toes. The paired leaves are bluish-green to light green in colour, and they are cylindrical and tubular. They are also often transparent. The plant's distinctive look is derived from the U-shaped fusion of its leaves at the base.

2. Depth: Apteryx succulents are often tiny, forming low mats or mounds when they grow in close groups. When fully grown, plants may stand three inches (7.5 cm) tall.

3. Dropping: Tiny, daisy-like blooms in shades of pink, yellow, or white are produced by Baby Toes. The plant's overall appeal is enhanced by the blossoms that grow out of the clefts between the paired leaves.

4. Modifications: Apteryx succulents have adapted to withstand harsh sunshine and little water to live in their natural habitat. Their distinct leaf structure facilitates effective water storage, which enables them to resist drought conditions.

Growth and Maintenance:

1. Light: Bright, indirect sunshine is ideal for baby toe growth. They can withstand brief periods of intense sunshine, but extended exposure may cause leaf burn.

2. Soil: These succulents need well-draining soil. A blend designed for succulents or cactus is appropriate.

3. Watering: Apteryx plants demand sparing irrigation since they evolved to live in dry climates. To avoid root rot, let the soil fully dry out in between waterings.
4.Temperature: They do best in warm weather and may tolerate light frost, but extended exposure to very cold temperatures should be avoided.

Uses:

1. Ornamental: Baby Toes are grown mainly for their aesthetic value, as they provide a

distinctive and eccentric element to container arrangements, succulent gardens, and rockeries.

2. Indoor Plants: Because Baby Toes are little, they may be cultivated inside as houseplants as long as they have access to enough light and soil that drains effectively.

3. Landscaping: You may use these succulents in water-conserving landscaping projects since they are a good fit for xeriscaping.

In conclusion, succulents known as Apteryx, or Baby Toes, are fascinating plants prized for their versatility and endearing look. They provide a touch of South African elegance to plant collections across the globe, whether they are used as little potted plants or as part of a larger succulent garden.

CHAPTER 3

CHOOSING THE IDEAL SUCCULENTS

Choosing the ideal succulents for your indoor or outdoor garden may be exciting and fulfilling, particularly for novices just starting in the world of plants. At first, the abundance of options may seem intimidating but have no fear—choosing the ideal succulents is a fun process that can be customized to your tastes and level of gardening expertise.

Succulents are a durable and low-maintenance plant that works well for beginners. The Echeveria, with its rosette-shaped leaves and vivid hues, is a great option. For people who are new to cultivating succulents, these hardy plants are a great choice since they grow in a variety of environments and need little maintenance. Because of their variety in size and colour, novices may try out various arrangements and give their green areas a creative touch.

The Haworthia, a little and endearing succulent with eye-catching geometric patterns on its leaves, is a distinctive twist. These plants can withstand reduced light levels and are thus well suited for indoor conditions. Haworthias may give an intriguing touch to your succulent collection with their unique forms and textures, igniting discussions about the fascinating world of desert plants.

Aloe vera is another unusual option; it is prized for both its therapeutic qualities and decorative appeal. The calming gel that aloe vera plants are renowned for may be used to soothe minor burns and skin irritations. This versatile succulent gives your collection a useful twist and proves that style and utility can live peacefully in your gardening pursuits.

If you're looking for variation, go no farther than the Sedum genus, which has a wide range of coloured and shaped succulents. From the ground-hugging Sedum spurium to the cascading Sedum burrito, popularly known as "Donkey Tail," each species provides a different visual experience. Because of their adaptability, novices may try out various growth patterns and customize their succulent choices to fit their preferred aesthetic.

For beginners looking for an eye-catching arrangement, another group of succulents that appeals is Crassula, with its characteristic piled leaves. The Jade Plant (Crassula ovata) is especially well-liked because of its association with wealth and good fortune. For those who are just beginning their succulent adventure, cultivating a jade plant is an appealing option as it not only gives an exquisite touch to your environment but also delivers good energy.

Furthermore, selecting the ideal succulents for your area requires taking into account a number of variables that affect their general health. The kinds of soil, amount of sunshine needed, and container choices all affect how well your succulent garden grows. To assist you in making wise choices, let's examine each of these facets in more detail.

Need for Sunlight:

Although it's well known that succulents may grow in direct sunshine, not all of them can. It is vital to comprehend the particular sunshine needs of the succulents that pique your attention. Certain succulents, such as Haworthia and Aloe Vera, require partially shaded or indirect light. Conversely, types like Sedum and Echeveria do well in direct sunshine. Examine how much sunshine your planned area receives, then choose succulents that will thrive in that environment.

Soil Categories:
Your succulents' health is greatly impacted by the kind of soil you use. In general, succulents want soil that drains properly to avoid soggy roots, which may cause root rot. To improve drainage, think about using a mixture that

contains elements like pumice, sand, or perlite. Customization based on the unique requirements of your selected succulents is possible when you make your succulent soil mix. Because succulents are native to dry climates, giving them a soil mixture that resembles those circumstances can boost their general health.

Options for Containers:
Not only is the container you choose for your succulents an aesthetic choice, but it also plays a vital role in their development. Diverse solutions for containers accommodate varying practical and aesthetic requirements. Because they breathe well and let excess moisture escape, terracotta pots are a popular choice for reducing root rot. Think of sleek ceramic or metal containers if you want a more contemporary style. Although they would need to be well sealed to avoid water damage, wooden containers can provide a rustic touch. Furthermore, drainage holes in containers are necessary to keep water from building up at the bottom and protect your succulents.

Pairing Attributes:
Consider how the colour, texture, and size of the succulents compliment one another when choosing your collection. Adding a striking layout gives your succulent garden a new level of complexity. For example, combining the upright structure of Sansevieria with the rosette form of Echeveria may result in a visually arresting and dynamic display. Adding interest to your succulent arrangement and showcasing the variety of the succulent world may be achieved by experimenting with opposing and complementary combinations.

Seasonal Differences:
Remember that depending on the season, succulents may need different care. They could need more sunshine and water during the growth season, and they might benefit from less irrigation during the dormant season. The long-term health of your succulents depends on you being aware of the seasonal differences and modifying your care regimen appropriately.

In conclusion, carefully weighing the needs for sunshine, kinds of soil, and container alternatives is necessary when selecting the proper succulents. You may construct a vibrant and eye-catching succulent garden by learning about the specific requirements of the succulents you have chosen and designing their surroundings appropriately. This individualized method guarantees a satisfying experience as you watch your succulents bloom in their carefully managed setting, regardless of your level of familiarity with succulents.

Also, it requires a careful balancing act between beauty, carelessness, and personal taste. With the wide variety of choices provided by Echeverias, Haworthias, Aloe Vera, Sedums, and Crassulas, even the most inexperienced gardener may select the ideal succulent partners. Cultivating these hardy plants will improve your living areas and provide a satisfying introduction to the world of succulents with a little trial and error and the delight of discovery.

CHAPTER 4

HOW TO TAKE CARE OF SUCCULENTS

Taking care of succulents is similar to taking care of a small, hardy garden that survives on neglect and requires very little maintenance. We set out on a voyage into the quirky world of these hardy plants, examining their particular demands and revealing the keys to their flourishing life, to learn the art of caring for succulents.

Timetables for Watering:

Imagine succulents, the camels of the plant world carrying water in their lush leaves for the days when the weather is dry. Succulent watering takes on the grace of a gentle ballet, a cadence between hydration and moderation. Consider the ebb and flow of soil moisture rather than imposing a rigid timetable. Allow the earth to tell its own stories, and water your succulents when its parched surface begins to murmur tales of thirst. It's an instinctive dance with nature that makes sure your succulents stay wet without being too fussy.

Needs for Sunlight:

Consider succulents as sun-lovers, lazing in the sun on a tropical beach like contented tourists. Although these plants love sunshine, they sometimes tolerate some shade. Play hide-and-seek with the sun so that your succulents may enjoy its radiance for a significant portion of the day. But do expose them to the occasional shade during the hot day, such as a sun hat, to avoid sunburn and make sure their vivid colours continue to be a tribute to their adventures in the sun.

Fundamental Upkeep:

Let's now explore the fundamental upkeep choreography, which involves caring for and appreciating your succulents like a ballet.

Consider it a day at the spa for your eco-friendly friends. Clear the area, use your fingers to gently remove the withering leaves, and let your succulents air. Assume the role of their stylist, enhancing their inherent attractiveness via shape and trimming. It's a time of healing love when you and your succulents communicate with one another via the language of loving touch.

The secret to this delicious symphony is not just regularity but also attention to care. Consider your succulents from an artistic perspective and pay attention to the little clues they provide. Maybe they want to chase the sun, or maybe they just want a splash of water or a change of scenery. Treat them with the inquisitiveness of a scientist venturing into unknown lands, appreciating the grace of their adaptations and coming to terms with their peculiarities.

Imagine this delicious route as a vibrant dance, an ongoing conversation with the natural world as you stroll down it. Allow your attention to be like a song, with every note reflecting the colourful life of these hardy plants. It's more than just a schedule; it's a dialogue that goes beyond the lines between caregiver and looked-after. It's a live, breathing relationship with your succulents.

Succulent maintenance is ultimately an artistic endeavour rather than a strict science. It's the skill of paying attention, paying attention, and adapting to these fascinating plant friends' particular demands. Thus, may your succulent voyage become a work of art, a painting adorned with the brushstrokes of sunlight, water, and thoughtful touch - a monument to the peaceful coexistence of human tending and the resiliency of nature.

Setting off on the fascinating adventure of caring for succulents reveals not only the beauty of these hardy plants but also the difficulties that may put even the most committed caregiver to the test. Two enemies stand out as we go across the lush terrain: the ever-present bug problem and the mild risk of overwatering. In this lush journey, we explore the complexities of these problems in more detail and provide a thorough guide to remedies that can strengthen your succulent sanctuary.

The Overwatering Problem:

Consider the careful balancing act of caring for your succulents as a ballet, where a mistake such as overwatering might ruin the elegant performance of your plant group. Even those who love succulents with the greatest of intentions might unintentionally overcare for their green friends.

Establishing a deliberate watering schedule is essential to reducing overwatering. Imagine yourself as a steward of the soil's mysteries, sensitive to its murmurs. As in the natural cycles of arid places where succulents flourish, let the topsoil dry out in between waterings. This deliberate drought-and-quench method makes sure your succulents get the moisture they need without falling victim to the dangers of soggy soil.

Think about the pot, the container that holds your succulent. Think of it as a caretaker in charge of preserving the delicate moisture balance. Select pots that have holes for drainage so that any extra water can drain out and the roots won't sit in water. With this little tweak, your pot becomes a haven, protecting your succulent from the dangers of over-moisture.

Furthermore, consider moisture meters to be your reliable partners in this undertaking. These clever instruments act as protectors, giving instantaneous information on the soil's moisture content. Think of them as navigational aids that will help you steer clear of the typical overwatering mistake and navigate the treacherous terrain of caring for succulents.

Insect Problems:

Succulents are a lush refuge, but they are not immune to pests that might ruin your other green friends' vibrant colours. Imagine tiny raiders gnawing, suctioning, or creeping their way into the centre of your cactus haven. But worry not a well-thought-out plan is prepared to fend against these plant enemies.

See yourself as a watchful guardian, scouring the lush boundaries of your delicious realm. Inspections regularly turn into your initial defence. Keep an eye out for obvious indicators of an infestation, such as discoloured leaves, sticky residue, or the small offenders themselves. Early identification prevents a little skirmish from turning into a full-scale invasion by laying the groundwork for a prompt response.

In this war against pests, natural friends play the part of brave defenders. Think of ladybugs as your little sparkling knights defending your plants from invading aphids. A botanical elixir called neem oil acts as your shield against pests, forming an impenetrable barrier without endangering the well-being of your succulents.

Quarantine becomes a tactical move in the event of a full-scale invasion. Envision a triage facility where sick succulents are kept apart from their healthy counterparts and given specialized treatment. Use organic insecticidal soaps to rid them of intruders while treating them gently. Imagine this as a hospital for your succulents, where you can precisely nurse them back to health.

In this pest-repelling strategy, companion planting develops as a harmonic coalition of botanical friends. Imagine fragrant plants such as rosemary and basil acting as watchful defenders, their alluring perfume naturally discouraging pests. It's a symphony of smells that keeps intruders at bay and cultivates a peaceful garden where partners and succulents live in harmony.

When you face these obstacles, see yourself as the protector of a succulent paradise rather than as its caregiver. Imagine a place where knowledge and attention to detail win against misfortunes, and where the dynamic interaction between your actions and your succulents' demands fosters a connection that goes beyond the typical one between a plant and its caregiver.

Your succulents become tough co-conspirators in the vast scheme of nature on this botanical voyage. Together, you strike the careful balance between dehydration and self-control, driving away pests with the dexterity of an experienced tactician. Imagine your succulent hideaway as a tribute to the artistic skill of nourishing life in all its complex forms and as a monument to the symbiotic dance between caregiver and cared for.

CHAPTER 5

METHODS OF PROPAGATING SUCCULENTS

An interesting part of growing succulents is propagation, which gives aficionados a chance to share the beauty of these hardy plants and grow their collection. Two straightforward and efficient propagation strategies that stand out among the others are leaf and stem cuttings.

Let's investigate the subtleties of each strategy as we dig into the fascinating realm of succulent growth.

Leaf Propagation:

The amazing trip a simple leaf takes to become a flourishing plant is one of the most captivating features of succulent leaf growth. Start this fascinating procedure by picking one of the parent succulent's healthy leaves. Choose a healthy, lush leaf that has reached full maturity for the maximum likelihood of success.

After selecting your leaf, carefully twist it off the main stem, making sure the split is clean and neither the leaf nor its base is harmed. In this journey of propagation, patience is essential. Let the severed leaf air dry for one or two days so that the wound heals into a callus. This important step reduces the possibility of infection and prepares the soil for a healthy rooting process.

Next, have a propagation medium ready that drains effectively. A specialist succulent mix or a combination of potting soil and perlite are excellent choices. Bury the callused end of the leaf in the ground just far enough to support it. During the first phases, the soil should be maintained somewhat wet; when roots begin to grow, the moisture content should be progressively reduced.

It's exciting to see little roots grow and finally small succulent babies. It's evidence of the tenacity of nature and the plant's natural capacity for regeneration. The tiny plantlet may be moved into its pot as it develops, beginning a new phase in its journey through succulents.

Stem Propagation:

While leaf propagation is magical, stem propagation tells a distinct, but no less fascinating, story. This method works especially well with succulents like Sedum or Echeveria types that have distinct stem structures.

Choosing a sound stem from the parent plant is the first step in the stem propagation process. Since a good start is essential, make sure the selected stem is free from injury and illness. Snip the stem right below a leaf node at the point on the stem where the leaves attach with a clean, sharp knife or pair of scissors.

As with leaf propagation, let the cut end of the stem air dry for a day or two. This drying time reduces the possibility of rot and prepares the soil for a strong root system. Plant the stem in a well-draining succulent mix when the cut end has hardened.

With stem propagation, you may produce many new plants from a single cutting, as opposed to leaf propagation, which starts with a single leaf. The callused end of the stem should be buried in the ground to provide the structure considerable support to avoid toppling. Similar to leaf propagation, start with a somewhat damp atmosphere and progressively change the watering as the roots grow.

It's satisfying to see the stem take root and grow into a self-sufficient succulent. After it has been rooted, you may move the plant into a separate pot, expanding your collection of succulents.

Conclusion: Taking Care of Succulents Using Magical Propagation

Propagation is a wonderful process in the world of succulent gardening that reveals the hardiness and flexibility of these fascinating plants. Every technique has its special appeal, whether you want to stem propagate, create several plants from a single cutting, or leaf propagate, watching as individual leaves turn into flourishing succulents.

Growing succulents makes you a custodian of growth and contributes to the natural world's cyclical beauty. The propagation process is a tribute to the miracles of life and the always-surprising world of succulents, from choosing the ideal leaf to seeing roots and leaves develop. Thus, embrace the art of propagation and let your succulent garden flourish as you create new life and beauty in the most captivating manner you can.

Furthermore, Learning these skills offers up a world of options for developing lush landscapes and fostering a closer relationship with nature, regardless of experience level in gardening. Let's explore various fascinating propagation techniques, providing detailed instructions and helpful hints for success.

1. Propagation of Water:

A fascinating technique that turns your house into a little aquatic paradise is water propagation. Start with cuttings from your favourite plants. Mint, pothos, and philodendron are great choices. Make sure a healthy stem is trimmed to a length of 4–6 inches, right below a node.

Ensure that the cutting is completely immersed in the water by placing it in a glass jar. To avoid bacterial development and stagnation, change the water every few days. You will see the miracle of roots growing out of the submerged node in a matter of weeks. Plant the cutting in soil after the roots are a few inches tall, and presto you've successfully propagated a new plant!

Tip: Use a clear jar to see the root development, which will make the procedure visually stunning.

2. Air Layering:

The method known as "air layering" seems complicated, but it is rather simple. Pick a robust branch from the plant of your choice, then cut a tiny, upward diagonal cut approximately a foot down from the tip. After carefully removing the bark to reveal the interior wood, apply rooting hormone dust to the injured region.

Make sure the wet sphagnum moss covers the incision by wrapping it over the exposed section. Using plastic wrap, firmly pack the moss to form a little greenhouse. Within the moss, roots will grow during the next several weeks. When they get strong enough, cut the branch that is below the root system and place it in the ground.

Tip: Don't be afraid to experiment with different plant species and choose branches with a decent thickness for effective air layering.

3. Division: Increase and Take Over

A traditional method of propagation, division works especially well for perennials like hostas and decorative grasses. The mature plant should first be dug up to accomplish division. Make sure every division has its own set of roots and shoots as you carefully separate the roots. By revitalizing the parent plant and producing new ones, this technique encourages healthy development.

When transplanting the divisions, make sure the soil bed is ready and give it plenty of water. Each division may grow into a strong, independent plant with the right care.

Tip: When plants are less stressed and more amenable to transplanting, divide them in the early spring or late autumn.

4. Cuttings from Leaves: Unlocking the Potential
of Fragile Beauty

A charming method for multiplying fragile and beautiful plants, such as begonias and succulents, is by leaf cuttings. Pick a healthy leaf to start with; it should be plump and damage-free. Make sure the leaf breaks cleanly away from the parent plant when you gently remove it.

Place the leaf with its base half buried in soil that drains nicely. To keep the soil wet, mist it often. A new plantlet will eventually grow from the leaf and small roots will show up from the area that is buried. You may move the newly formed plant to its permanent location after it is well-established.

Tip: When it comes to leaf cuttings, patience is essential. Try not to disturb them when they are just starting to develop.

5. Grafting: Botanical Fusion at Its Finest

Grafting is a propagation method that verges on artistic horticulture. To generate a single, harmonious creature, the tissues of two separate plants are combined. Even though it seems complicated, it may be a rewarding talent with sufficient practice.

Choose a chosen scion (the plant you want to reproduce) and a healthy rootstock plant. Make sure the scion and rootstock fit tightly together by making a neat, diagonal incision on each of them. To create an airtight seal, fasten them with rubber bands or grafting tape. You will see the birth of a plant that best represents the traits of both parents when the tissues fuse.

Tip: Start with appropriate plant kinds and progressively hone your abilities; mastering grafting may take some time.

In the world of plant propagation, these methods are like the keys that open a colourful, diverse garden. Try out these techniques, take note of their distinct qualities, and see how your gardening abilities develop along with your expanding group of green friends.

CHAPTER 6

ARRANGING SUCCULENTS IN GARDENS AND CONTAINERS

Making a captivating succulent arrangement is more than just gardening; it's an artistic undertaking that allows you to construct a tapestry of hues, textures, and forms. Let your imagination go wild when you arrange succulents whether in gardens or containers just the way succulent leaves do. This investigation ought to be a unique experience that deviates from the norm. Here, we go into a comprehensive guide that offers inspiring suggestions for turning your succulent arrangements into stunning living artwork.

Celebrate Diversity:
Succulents come in an amazing variety of forms and hues. Try experimenting with vivid reds, purples, and blues to break off from the traditional green colour scheme. Combine

trailing sedums with rosette-shaped echeverias to create an eye-catching, diverse design. This variety gives your succulent arrangement more visual appeal while showcasing the diversity of nature.

The Filler, Thriller, and Spiller Method:

Consider using the thriller, filler, and spiller approach when arranging containers. Choose a striking succulent to serve as the "thriller", an attention-grabbing focal point that steals the show. Plant "filler" succulents all around it to create a harmonious blend of sizes and forms. For extra drama, let trailing succulents function as "spillers," tumbling over the container's edges. This methodical technique guarantees a visually pleasing and dynamic layout.

Vertical Succulent Gardening:

Create a vertical garden to add flair to your succulent arrangement. Build a multi-tiered succulent paradise by repurposing pallets or wall-mounted planters. This gives your arrangement more dynamic appeal while also making the most of the available space. Combine succulents with different growth patterns to create a stunning vertical garden.

Arrangements Based on Themes:

Using a theme can let you include narrative into your succulent arrangement. Let your imagination take you to a fantasy garden or an oasis in the desert. To further the concept, add little figurines, ornamental stones, or unusual containers. Your succulent display may become a living piece of art with a well-crafted narrative that invites viewers to interact with the tale it presents.

The Elegance of Terrarium:

A terrarium will add a touch of sophistication to your arrangement of succulents. Select a glass container that allows you to see the microenvironment within in all directions. For further visual appeal, layer several sand or gravel textures. To create a contemplative and engaging terrarium environment, use succulents that vary in height and shape.

Magic Colour Gradient:

Arrange succulents in a colour gradient to create a captivating arrangement. In the center, start with the brightest, boldest colours you can find, then work your way outward to softer tones. This not only displays your creative ability but also directs the viewer's gaze over a variety of hues, elevating your arrangement to the center of attention in any area.

Adaptable Containers:

For your succulents, consider using unusual containers rather than just standard pots. Old boots, wooden boxes, and vintage teacups may all give your arrangement a unique twist. This not only demonstrates your upcycling awareness and environmental care, but it also gives your succulent arrangement a surprising touch of charm.

Summertime Glimmer:
Celebrate the seasonal changes by modifying your arrangement of succulents. Fall is a great time to introduce bright, warm tones with flower-like rosette-shaped succulents. Choose types with chilly tones that resemble frost in the winter. This dynamic design guarantees that your succulent arrangement will always be eye-catching and fresh.

Bonsai Happiness:
Discover the craft of bonsai with tiny succulents. Pruning and shaping these hardy plants into little trees results in a visually arresting combination of two very different horticultural traditions. Bonsai succulents demonstrate your commitment to the painstaking art of cultivation in addition to adding a touch of refinement.

Silhouettes at Sunset:

Succulents may be arranged to resemble the warm light of dusk to capture the enchantment of a sunset. To simulate the sun setting on the horizon, arrange succulents in a circular pattern using vibrant reds, oranges, and purples. This arrangement gives your room a peaceful feeling while also showcasing your love of the outdoors.

Your creativity is the only restriction when it comes to the wide world of succulent arranging. Allow your imagination to go wild as you build a refined bonsai masterpiece or a charming fairy garden. Because of their versatility and distinctive qualities, succulents are the ideal medium for your botanical artwork. So start your gardening adventure and let your arrangement of succulents serve as a live example of your inventiveness. Give each succulent a chance to tell a tale, and see as your arrangement develops into a colourful work of art that brings life and beauty into your room.

Moreover, whether you're creating displays for your home, business, or yard, you need to have a creative flair and an excellent eye for design. The skill of fusing several species whether they be plants, artwork, or interior design elements can create a room that is both visually beautiful and harmonious.

Let's begin with plants, which infuse every environment with vitality and life. Combining several plant types may result in a rich, vibrant show. Think about the difference between tiny, blooming plants and towering, leafy ones. The arrangement gains depth via the contrast in heights, which directs the viewer's gaze in different directions.

It's critical to comprehend the requirements of each participating plant species to establish equilibrium. Take into account elements like the need for sunshine, preferred water, and development trends. Plants with comparable requirements grow better when grouped, making for a display that is both colourful and healthy.

Another essential component in making visually appealing arrangements is texture. Combine plants with a variety of leaf textures, such as glossy, matte, rough, and smooth. This variety gives the display a captivating haptic aspect. For example, pairing succulents with delicate, feathery ferns produces an enticing contrast that begs to be touched as well as looked at.

A display's overall aesthetics are greatly influenced by colour. Even while monochromatic arrangements may be sophisticated, adding a spectrum of hues can make the space seem vibrant and energetic. When choosing plants, keep in mind the colour wheel. Complementary hues, which are opposite one another on the wheel, may accentuate one another's brightness when arranged together.

Think outside of the box while arranging plants. Try experimenting with unusual containers like hanging planters, colourful pottery, or old-fashioned boxes. The selection of containers enhances the display's overall originality by adding another level of visual intrigue.

Let's go beyond plants and investigate the world of artwork and ornamental accents. Putting disparate works of art together in a way that flows demands careful consideration. Start by thinking of a unifying theme or colour scheme for the artworks. Subject matter, style, or even emotional tone might serve as the foundation for this topic.

Combining several art mediums, such sculptures, paintings, and photos, may give a show more depth. To direct the viewer's attention and establish focus points, think about grouping smaller pieces. Try experimenting with asymmetry to offer a surprise and dynamic aspect while departing from conventional symmetrical arrangements.

Enhancing the emotional effect of the exhibit may be achieved by adding nostalgic artifacts or handcrafted crafts. These components not only add to the arrangement's originality but also provide the room with a warm, individual feel.

Lighting is an effective technique that may significantly improve any display's aesthetic appeal. To add depth and emphasize certain components, try experimenting with various light sources, such as floor lamps, table lamps, or string lights. The arrangement is more appealing because of the depth of intricacy added by the interaction of light and shadow.

When setting up displays, take into account the surrounding area. The environment, whether it be a living room, workplace, or garden, affects the display's overall mood. Make sure the layout blends in seamlessly and seems well at home with the existing architecture and furnishings.

Combining diverse types of plants takes on a new meaning in outdoor environments. Think about the temperature, sunshine exposure, and the natural scenery. Group plants that have similar requirements together to create microenvironments. For example, shade-loving ferns under larger trees or sun-loving succulents soaking up the brilliant sunshine.

In summary, the skill of creative arrangement and exhibition includes the tasteful blending of many species, whether they are plants, artwork, or interior design items. Understanding the properties of each element and experimenting with different combinations can help you create visually arresting displays that draw attention and instill a feeling of harmony and beauty in the room. So, go ahead and let your imagination run wild as you set out to turn your surroundings into a visually stunning painting.

CHAPTER 7

ALL-INCLUSIVE GUIDES TO SUCCULENT MAINTENANCE FOR BEGINNERS

Because of their compelling beauty and variety of shapes, succulents have come to represent the tenacity of nature. It's crucial for novices entering the realm of succulent maintenance to realize that these plants need a certain kind of care. We will examine the nuances of succulent care in this comprehensive book, which includes advice on soil concerns, watering techniques, and setting up the ideal habitat. A troubleshooting section also helps beginners overcome typical obstacles.

Selecting the Appropriate Setting:

Originating in dry areas, succulents have evolved to flourish in certain environments. The first step towards effective succulent care is choosing the right setting. Even while certain succulents can withstand intense sunshine, it's important to find a healthy balance. When growing a diversified collection, it is particularly important to aim for bright, indirect light. Remember that extended exposure to strong sunlight might cause an ugly sunburn that can harm the plant in general.

Choosing The Most Suitable Soil:

The secret to taking care of succulents is to mix the soil just so. The majority of succulents hate soggy conditions, thus their soil must drain well. This may be accomplished using a homemade combination of potting soil, perlite, or coarse sand, or with a professionally purchased succulent mix. The idea is to let extra water escape so that root rot, a typical problem for lovers of succulents, doesn't occur.

Watering Sufficiently:

A vital part of taking care of succulents is learning how to water them properly. Here, the proverb "less is more" is very appropriate. Because their leaves hold water, succulents need regular yet thorough watering. When watering, make sure the water reaches the root zone and allows the soil to dry fully in between treatments. Reduce the chance of fungal problems by not overwatering the leaves by using a watering can with narrow spouts.

- **Solving Problems Encountered In Succulents Gardening:**

Even the most careful plant caretakers may run into problems. This section on troubleshooting is meant to assist novices in recognizing and resolving typical issues:

1. Drooping or Yellowing Leaves:

 Causes: Excessive watering.
Solution: Reduce watering until the soil dries up, modifying your schedule as necessary.

2. Wrinkled or Shrivelled Leaves:

Causes: Insufficient watering
Solution: Increasing the frequency of watering will ensure that the soil is adequately hydrated.

3. Black or Soft Rotting Spots:

Causes: Soil that is too wet causes root rot.
Solution: Take out the plant, cut off any impacted roots, and plant again in soil that drains well.

4. Stunting and Weak Growth:

Causes: Inadequate sunshine.
Solution: Move the succulent to a more sunny location where it will get at least 6 hours of indirect sunlight every day.

5. White Cotton-Like Substance on Leaves:

Causes: Mealybugs or aphids.
Solution: Use a solution of water and mild soap to clean the afflicted regions. Consider using

insecticidal soap or neem oil in extreme situations.

Finally, the skill of succulent care develops through time and observation. By providing insights into the complex world of succulent care from comprehending their native environment to resolving frequent problems this book seeks to assist novices. Since every succulent is different, you may create a bright and flourishing succulent refuge in your house by attending to their specific demands. I hope your succulents grow and inspire you to appreciate the wonders of nature every day.

- **Recognizing and Managing Stress, Illnesses, and Obstacles in Succulents**

Although growing succulents is a rewarding endeavour, there are some difficulties involved. For succulent caregivers, identifying the warning symptoms of illnesses, stress, and other conditions is crucial. We will examine the subtleties of succulent health in this comprehensive guide, identifying the subliminal clues that can indicate underlying issues. You can make sure your succulents flourish in their distinctive, alluring beauty by being aware of these symptoms and taking proactive measures to resolve them.

1. Overwatering Problems:

A typical mistake made by succulent fans is overwatering, which may have disastrous results. Yellowing or transparent leaves are indicative of overwatering, which suffocates the roots with too much moisture. A bad smell and soft, mushy stems are indicative of root rot, which is common in wet environments. Reduce the frequency of your waterings and let the soil dry up fully in between applications to prevent overwatering. Make sure the soil drains properly to avoid standing rainwater around the roots.

2. The Underwatering Dilemma:

On the other hand, stress from underwatering may cause shrivelled, wrinkled leaves and reduced development in succulents. The plant may show a smaller size and change shape to save water. Increasing the frequency of watering will help solve under-watering as long as the soil is fully saturated after each session. Because different succulent plants have varying levels of drought tolerance, pay attention to their unique requirements.

3. Fighting Burns:

Even though they are hardy plants, succulents may become sunburned if they are left in direct sunlight for extended periods. Brown or discoloured areas on the leaves, especially those that face the sun, are signs of the disease. Sunburn may be avoided by gradually acclimating to direct sunlight and by seeking shade during the warmest times of the day. Determine the amount of sunshine your succulents need, then adjust their location to get the ideal ratio of light exposure to protection.

4. The Problem of Leggy Growth:

Lack of sunlight may cause lanky growth, which is characterized by elongated stems and widely separated leaves. This extended growth style is shown by succulents as a means of compensating for insufficient exposure to light. Move your succulents to a brighter location where they may get at least 6 hours of indirect sunshine each day to correct lanky development. Trim lanky branches to promote more branched development.

5. Handling Challenges from Bacteria and Fungi:

Succulents are prone to bacterial or fungal infections that generate soft, mushy leaves with discoloured or black areas. Remove afflicted leaves as soon as possible, improve airflow around the plants, and use fungicides or antimicrobial treatments if infections continue. Plant spacing correctly and avoiding overhead watering are two preventive methods that may lower the danger of bacterial and fungal problems.

6. Invading Pests:

Succulents may suffer from infestations of pests like mealybugs, aphids, and spider mites, which can be detected by white, cotton-like material on their leaves, little webs, or visible insects. Wipe afflicted areas with a solution of water and mild soap to combat bugs. Neem oil or insecticidal soap might be useful for severe infestations. Check your succulents often for indications of insect activity, and respond quickly to save more damage.

7. Nutritional Deficiencies:
Even while succulents don't eat a lot, they may sometimes show signs of nutritional inadequacies, such as yellowing leaves, particularly when they first emerge. During the growth season, use a balanced fertilizer while following suggested dilution rates to avoid

overfertilization. Optimizing nutrient uptake requires tailoring your fertilization strategy to your succulents'unique requirements.

8. Environmental Stressors:

Stress may be caused by abrupt changes in temperature, drafts, or relocation because succulents react to environmental changes. Wilting, leaf drop, or colour changes are a few possible indicators. Assimilate your succulents gradually so they may adjust to their new surroundings without experiencing excessive stress. Keep them safe from excessive temperature swings and provide them with a steady atmosphere so they may develop consistently.

In conclusion, we have looked at the symptoms of illnesses, stress, and other problems that caretakers may face as we work to uncover the mysteries of succulent health. Knowing these subtleties, from the dangers of overwatering to the complexities of dealing with pests, enables succulent fans to give their cherished plants the focused care they need. Taking a proactive stance when it comes to the health of your succulents sets you on the path to growing robust, flourishing plants that will adorn your area with their distinct allure. May the growth of your succulent collection serve as a testament to the benefits of careful and knowledgeable maintenance.

CHAPTER 8

HOW TO TAKE CARE OF SUCCULENTS DURING DIFFERENT SEASONS

Succulent maintenance is similar to caring for a landscape full of small, hardy sculptures. Even though these resistant plants are renowned for their capacity to flourish in dry environments, they nonetheless need extra care over the seasonal transition. Join us as we take a seasonal tour around the world of succulents and learn about the subtleties involved in taking care of these extraordinary plants.

Awakening of Spring:

Sunlight is what succulents want when they emerge from their winter hibernation and the world around them explodes with colour. Since spring is a time of rebirth, your succulents hunger for that energizing sunshine. Make sure they get the early light since it is kinder and won't burn them.

Another ideal season for development is the spring. If your succulent has outgrown its existing location, think about repotting it. The aeration required for strong root growth may be obtained from a soil mixture that drains efficiently. Use water sparingly, letting the soil dry up in between applications. This is also the time of year to propagate; cut off a healthy leaf and see a new succulent life form.

Summer Heatwave:

Ahh, summertime, when even the hardiest succulents are put to the test. It is essential to protect your succulents from scorching sun rays while the sun is shining above. To avoid sunburn, give them some afternoon shade or relocate them to an area with filtered light.

In the summer, watering turns into a delicate dance. Succulents love a drink in the intense heat, even if they are champions of drought resistance. To reduce evaporation, water in the early morning or late evening, and take care not to let them sit in moist soil.

If your succulents are outside, watch out for pests that are trying to escape the heat. Unwanted guests may be kept at bay with a little mist of neem oil, keeping your succulents the stars of the summertime show.

Fall Peacefulness:

Succulents smoothly transition into fall when the temperature drops and the leaves change to a kaleidoscope of warm colours. Now is the time to get them ready for the approaching cold of winter. Reduce the frequency of watering the soil gradually to enable it to dry out more fully. Succulents slow down their development in response to minute variations in the length of sunshine.

Aim to move outside succulents inside prior to the onset of frost. All they'll need to get the light they still need on these shorter days is a sunny windowsill. Autumn may provide a second opportunity for propagation before winter hibernation if you reside in a warmer area.

Dormancy for Winter:

Succulents enter a dormant state in response to the quiet calm of winter. Refrain from fertilizing; this is not the season for aggressive development. Use water sparingly, making sure the soil is kept just wet enough to avoid drying out and to discourage rot.

Succulents inside could want a break in a colder spot, away from drafty windows. If your outdoor succulents withstand the winter cold, cover their roots with a layer of mulch to act as insulation.

Winter considerations go beyond just taking care of the plant physically. Welcome the warm ambiance with décor inspired by succulents, honouring their resilient nature against the wintry scenery.

Overall Seasonal Advice:

Throughout the year, pay attention to the look of your succulents. They use little cues to express what they require. When leaves have a glossy, plump appearance, they are happy. They may need to be hydrated if they begin to seem wrinkled or discoloured.

Never forget that appreciating and comprehending their natural cycles is essential to culinary success. Although these hardy plants can withstand a wide range of circumstances, modifying your maintenance schedule to correspond with the seasonal shifts guarantees a vibrant, all-year succulent haven.

In summary, taking care of succulents is like dancing with nature in harmony each season creating its special tune. Your succulents will repay you with an enthralling display of resiliency and beauty as you negotiate the ups and downs of the botanical symphony, demonstrating once again that even the smallest of plants can impart important knowledge about growth and adaptability.

Adjustments Needed During Extreme Weather Conditions.

Due to their eye-catching variety of forms and hues, succulents are now valued additions to many homes and landscapes. Although these hardy plants are well-known for their capacity to flourish in dry environments, harsh weather may present difficulties that need certain adjustments to maintenance. To protect these unusual botanical marvels, succulent fans must adjust their methods whether they are subjected to frigid weather, intense heat waves, or erratic storms.

Succulents generally face the worst circumstances during the scorching summer months. To combat the unrelenting heat, think about offering some relief with well-placed shade. Even though these plants love the sun, they may avoid sunburn and keep their vivid colours by taking a vacation from the noon heat. Consider it a delicious power nap that will help them recover before the sun's next fury. Another game-changer is mulching the area surrounding the succulents' bases to lower soil temperature and preserve valuable moisture.

In intense heat, water the succulents' elixir of life takes center stage. Strive for a balance between moderation and hydration. The secret is to water deeply and seldom. Allow the soil to dry out in between waterings rather than dousing it with water like you would with an afternoon shower. This avoids the dreaded root rot, a bad effect of overwatering, and matches their natural environment. Think about covering the topsoil with a layer of gravel or stones for an additional layer of protection. This promotes moisture retention in addition to improving the appearance.

Succulent lovers need to turn their attention from sunscreen to thermal blankets when the seasons change and winter's chill sets in. Since they are native to dry climates, succulents are not suited for extended exposure to below-freezing temperatures. A quick and easy fix is to bring potted succulents indoors or into a covered location during the coldest nights. Consider it like covering them with a warm blanket to protect them from the chilly chill in the air.

Additionally, think about changing the watering schedule. In contrast to the busy growth season, winter calls for a more relaxed strategy. Reducing the frequency of irrigation will help the soil dry up more completely. It's crucial to keep a careful balance, however. Even though they prefer drier environments, succulents still need some water to get through the winter doldrums. When it's time to fill their thirst, a watchful eye and a finger dipped in dirt may be trusted guides.

Succulents demonstrate their resilience in the face of erratic weather, but a considerate caregiver may provide an additional degree of protection. Rain wind, and storms always call for a preventative approach. Make sure your drainage system is in place if the prediction calls for a lot of rain to avoid soggy soil. To prevent water from collecting near the base of potted succulents, think about shifting them to protected areas or gently raising them.

Wind is a dangerous enemy that is often disregarded. Succulents are used to windy weather, but too much wind may cause bodily harm and dehydration. Using natural windbreaks, such as ornamental pebbles or additional potted plants arranged thoughtfully around your succulent refuge, is a creative adjustment. This not only provides some artistic flare but also protects the fragile succulents from the wind.

Adaptation is key to the ongoing story of succulent care. The skill is in watching, adjusting, and refining the care regimen in light of the particular difficulties presented by severe weather. It's a symphony in which every note advances the health of these fascinating plant companions, a dance between the environment and the gardener.

To sum up, adapting succulent care for harsh weather is a complex and interesting task. Every modification is essential to the succulent story, from delivering a warm winter sanctuary to shading throughout the sweltering summers to bracing for erratic storms. It is a tale of tenacity, flexibility, and the deft balancing act between the gardener's gentle touch and the capricious character of the natural world. With knowledge, observation, and a little bit of imagination, set off on this botanical journey, and watch your succulents flourish despite any weather-related difficulties.

CHAPTER 9

SUCCULENT SUCCESSFUL STORIES

Beginners are encouraged to start their succulent journeys by the wealth of success stories and experiences that abound in the fascinating world of succulents, where persistence meets beauty. These are stories of strong people who found comfort, happiness, and a deep feeling of achievement in caring for these amazing floral marvels in addition to robust plants.

Clara, a beginner lover of succulents, opens one such story. Her balcony used to be a lifeless zone, aching for something more. She chose to turn her plain concrete canvas into a colourful succulent haven because she was drawn to the appeal of succulents. With a few hardy plants and some rudimentary information, Clara set out on her quest.

Trial and error characterized the early going. Her learning curve included occasional inadvertent sunburns, over- and under-waterings, and other mishaps. Clara, however, learned to adapt and read the small cues from her succulents after each failure. It was important to recognize the particular requirements of every succulent species that graced her balcony in addition to giving them water and sunshine.

Walking around her succulent paradise one day, Clara came across an intriguing arrangement that seemed to defy gravity. A hanging planter with succulents cascading down it like a live waterfall, producing an amazing sight. She was curious about this gravity-defying exhibition, so she asked other aficionados for guidance, which helped her to discover the solution.

Clara wanted to try something new, spurred on by the inventiveness of her succulent community. She styled a hanging planter with a variety of trailing succulents that she had carefully chosen. Over many weeks, her invention took root and blossomed, turning her balcony into a living beauty that attracted the attention of both neighbours and onlookers.

Clara's tale is but one of several strands that are interwoven to create a sumptuous picture of luscious achievement. These stories not only honour the plants' tenacity but also demonstrate the transformational potential of developing a relationship with nature. Succulents are partners on a voyage of self-discovery and progress for many fans, surpassing their status as just decorative plants.

Succulents are becoming hope symbols in the middle of concrete-dominated metropolitan settings. Consider the tale of Alex, who lives in a city full of busy streets and buildings. Alex created a succulent haven on a tiny apartment balcony despite its lack of natural light and space.

Alex made a beautiful green wall with a variety of succulents using vertical gardening methods. A haven from the mayhem below, the once-boresome balcony was transformed into an urban sanctuary. Alex overcame the limitations of city life and developed a fresh love for succulent design via thoughtful selection and arrangement.

Succulent lovers' travels aren't confined to their areas. Meet Sarah, the educator who included succulents in her lesson plans. Sarah included succulents in her lesson plan to inspire her pupils with the beauties of nature. As they took care of their little succulent gardens, the kids not only gained knowledge about plant biology but also acquired a feeling of responsibility.

The effects were felt outside of the classroom. Succulent excitement spread across the school community as a result of the inspiration parents and coworkers received to follow suit. For the kids as well as the school's overall ethos, the succulents came to represent progress.

Imagine a succulent garden that is illuminated by the twilight hours of the setting sun, creating shadows that play with the leaves. Think of a Haworthia's beautiful patterns as if they were a piece of natural art. These show a world where the commonplace becomes remarkable; they are more than simply candid photographs.

Take inspiration from these tales as you set out on your succulent trip. A flourishing plant is not the only indicator of success when growing succulents, learning, and having fun are all important aspects of the process. Succulents enable you to create your success narrative, whether you're revamping a balcony, taking on urban problems, or inspiring awe in a classroom.

Every leaf on a succulent plant has a narrative to tell, and these tales are evidence of the beauty that results from a combination of tenacity and passion. Therefore, take out your watering can and join the expanding group of succulent aficionados who are transforming common areas into remarkable displays of the majesty and tenacity of nature. Your delicious success story is there, waiting to be developed and told to the world.

www.ingramcontent.com/pod-product-compliance
Lightning Source LLC
Chambersburg PA
CBHW070805260726
48660CB00005B/1706